W9-BWU-789

ANIMAL KINGDOM CLASSIFICATION

LOBSTERS, CRABS & OTHER CRUSTACEANS

By Daniel Gilpin

Content Adviser: Jonathan Green, Ph.D.,
Professor of Biology, Department of Biological, Chemical and
Physical Science, Roosevelt University, Chicago

Science Adviser: Terrence E. Young Jr., M.Ed., M.L.S.,
Jefferson (Louisiana) Public School System

First published in the United States in 2006 by
Compass Point Books
3109 West 50th St., #115
Minneapolis, MN 55410

ANIMAL KINGDOM CLASSIFICATION–CRUSTACEANS
was produced by

David West Children's Books
7 Princeton Court
55 Felsham Road
London SW15 1AZ

Copyright © 2006 David West Children's Books

All rights reserved. No part of this book may be reproduced without written permission from the publisher. The publisher takes no responsibility for the use of any of the materials or methods described in this book, nor for the products therof.

Designer: David West
Editors: Gail Bushnell, Anthony Wacholtz, Kate Newport
Page Production: James Mackey

Visit Compass Point Books on the Internet at
www.compasspointbooks.com
or e-mail your request to
custserv@compasspointbooks.com

Library of Congress Cataloging-in-Publication Data
Gilpin, Daniel.
  Lobsters, crabs & other crustaceans / by Daniel Gilpin.
    p. cm.—(Animal kingdom classification)
  Includes bibliographical references.
  ISBN 0-7565-1612-9 (hard cover)
  1. Crustacea—Juvenile literature. 2. Lobsters—Juvenile literature. 3. Crabs—Juvenile literature. I. Title: Lobsters, crabs, and other crustaceans. II. Title. III. Series.
  QL437.2G55 2006
  595.3—dc22   2005029180

PHOTO CREDITS:
Abbreviations: t-top, m-middle, b-bottom, r-right, l-left, c-center.

Front cover, tr and bl, Corbis Images; 3, 4–5, 6t, Corbis Images; 6b (Nature Shell 0496), budgetstockphoto.com; 7r, NASA; 8t, OAR/National Undersea Research Program (NURP); 8cr, Oxford Scientific; 8b, George Harrison; 9tl, Asther Lau; 9tr, E. Williams, OAR/National Undersea Research Program (NURP); 11b, Mark Jensen; 14l, Oxford Scientific; 15r, John Archer; 16t, Amanda Rohde; 16b, Jose Acosta; 17t, 17l, 17r, Oxford Scientific; 18t, Oxford Scientific; 18c, OAR/National Undersea Research Program (NURP); 19r, Oxford Scientific; 20t, 20b, Oxford Scientific; 21l, OAR/National Undersea Research Program (NURP); 21r, Oxford Scientific; 22t, 22c, 22r, Oxford Scientific; 24t, 24b, Oxford Scientific; 25t, Oxford Scientific; 26t, Angela Bell; 26b, Oxford Scientific; 27t, Jurgen Freund; 28t, Stefan Klein; 28l, Dan Schmitt; 28c, OAR/National Undersea Research Program (NURP); 30t, Oxford Scientific; 30b, Jamie Hall; 31t, 31b, Oxford Scientific; 32t, 32b, Oxford Scientific; 33t, Oxford Scientific; 33b, Mark Jensen; 34t, Oxford Scientific; 34b, Rene Mansi; 35t, 35b, Oxford Scientific; 36t, 36b, Oxford Scientific; 37t, 37b, Oxford Scientific; 38t, 38b, Oxford Scientific; 39t, Keith Duford; 39b, Oxford Scientific; 40t, Dennis Oblander; 40b, Oxford Scientific; 41t, Oxford Scientific; 42l, Paul Cowan, 42r, Greg Nicholas, 42b, Joanna Bolick; 43t, E. Wenner, OAR/National Undersea Research Program (NURP); S. Carolina Mar. Resources Institute; 43b, Oxford Scientific

Every effort has been made to contact copyright holders of any material reproduced in this book. Any omissions will be rectified in subsequent printings if notice is given to the publishers.

With special thanks to the models: Felix Blom, Tucker Bryant, and Margaux Monfared.

Front cover: Hermit crab
Opposite: Hermit crab

ANIMAL KINGDOM CLASSIFICATION

LOBSTERS, CRABS & OTHER CRUSTACEANS

Daniel Gilpin

COMPASS POINT BOOKS ✦ MINNEAPOLIS, MINNESOTA

TABLE OF CONTENTS

INTRODUCTION

Crustaceans are the insects of the sea. Like insects, they have a tough, jointed exoskeleton and are numerous, widespread, and adapatable. Crustaceans have so much in common with their land equivalents because they are distantly related to them. Both groups belong to the phylum Arthropoda, a grouping in scientific classification that also includes arachnids, such as spiders, and scorpions. Unlike other arthropods, crustaceans all have gills and most live in the sea. They include lobsters, crabs, prawns, and barnacles. The only true land crustaceans are sow bugs.

HARD CASE

Lobsters include some of the biggest of all invertebrates. Like other crustaceans, they have a tough protective shell that covers virtually all of the body. Although this shell is hard, it has many different joints that allow for great flexibility. Crustacean shells are called exoskeletons because they support the body like our own internal skeleton does.

TYPES OF CRUSTACEANS

HERMIT CRAB

More than 38,000 species of crustaceans have been identified, and they come in a huge range of forms. Some, such as lobsters and prawns, are familiar, but others look quite bizarre.

THE PINCER MOVEMENT

The creatures most of us recognize as crustaceans make up a group called the decapods. Decapods include lobsters, crabs, prawns, and shrimps. The word *decapod* means "10 feet" in Latin. A more accurate name would mean "10 limbs," since many decapods have only eight feet, the other two limbs ending in pincers.

TEEMING HORDES

Other crustaceans fall into one of eight groups. Sow bugs make up the only group that lives on land. The best-known group is made up of barnacles, which spend their adult lives fixed to one spot. Copepods are microscopic and make up a larger group with around 5,000 species. They live as plankton in the ocean along with another group, the mystacocarids. Members of the seed shrimps and cephalocarids groups are a little larger, although still very tiny. The other two groups are the fish lice and the branchiopods.

BARNACLES

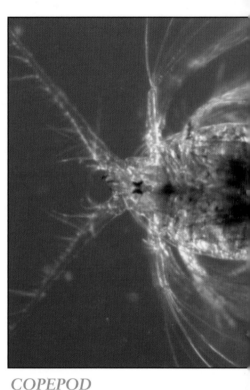
COPEPOD

GHOST CRAB

HINGE BEAK SHRIMP

SOW BUGS

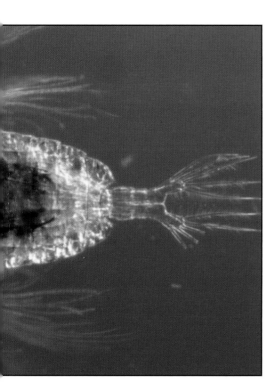

ROCK LOBSTER

ARROW CRABS

These little sea creatures look more like spiders than crabs. Their sticklike limbs can be three times as long as their bodies. Arrow crabs are scavengers that come out at night. They have eight legs and two other limbs that end in pincers. Although most of the food they eat is already dead, they sometimes use their long pincers to pull feather duster worms from their tubes and feed on them. Most arrow crabs are small but the largest can have leg spans of up to 6 inches (15 centimeters) long.

Many species of arrow crab live on coral reefs.

WHERE CRUSTACEANS LIVE

Most crustaceans live in water and the vast majority live in the sea. Some spend their lives on the bottom, while others swim in open water. A few even live in the sediments of the seabed itself.

LAND LUBBER

Sow bugs are the only crustaceans that spend their lives out of water.

IN THE OCEAN

Some marine crustaceans are built for swimming and others for walking. The walkers include crabs and lobsters. Lobsters spend most of their time on the sea bottom, although they can also swim short distances. Crabs walk over the seabed, too, but some also come out of the water onto mudflats and beaches. Crustacean swimmers include prawns and shrimps. Most live relatively solitary lives, but a few species form massive swarms. Krill, which live in the icy waters off Antarctica, belong to this group. Smaller swimmers, such as copepods, drift through the open ocean as plankton. Cephalocarids burrow in the mud on the sea bottom.

SHORE THING

Some crabs spend long periods of time out of water and many feed on land. However, they all have to return to the sea to breed.

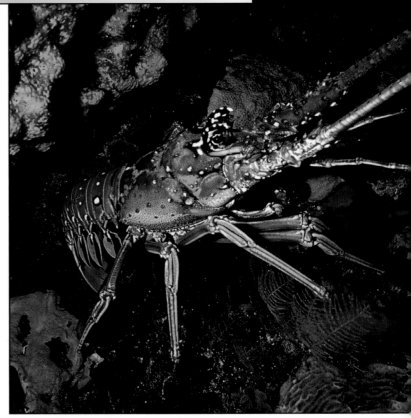

UNDERWATER WALKER

Most lobsters live on the seabed, although some inhabit coral reefs. Many spend the daylight hours hidden away from predators in a favorite crevice and only emerge at night to feed.

OTHER HABITATS

Sow bugs live on land under rotting logs and in leaf litter. Sometimes they even find their way into houses. Their close relative, the sand hopper, lives on beaches.

Some crustaceans, such as crayfish, inhabit freshwater. Brine shrimps live in salty lakes where few other creatures can survive.

DEEP SEA PRAWN

Many deep sea crustaceans are red. This is because red light is absorbed before it reaches deep water, making red creatures invisible there.

MOBILE HOMES

As adults, most barnacles live settled lives attached to rocks and filtering food from the seawater that passes by. A few, however, find themselves in perpetual motion. Barnacle larvae attach themselves to particular solid objects that they come across. Usually that object is sitting on or part of the seabed, but occasionally it is the shell or skin of another animal.

Sometimes barnacles attach themselves to whales. This does not harm the whale in any way.

CRUSTACEAN BODY PLAN

The word *crustacea* means "the shelled ones." This name describes the most obvious feature of these invertebrates, but it is their mouthparts and antennae that define them and set them apart from other arthropods.

IDENTIFYING FEATURES

All crustaceans have two pairs of antennae and three pairs of feeding appendages, which make up their mouthparts. Another feature they share is gills. Even sow bugs have these, despite the fact that they live on land. Sow bugs live in damp places and keep their gills constantly moist. Oxygen passes into the water covering them before it is absorbed by the gills into the body. Most crustacean larvae are oval and without segments.

Antenna

SEGMENTS AND APPENDAGES

Although a crustacean's shell has many sections, its body is divided into three main parts: the head, thorax, and abdomen. In most crustaceans, the head and thorax are fused into one structure called the cephalothorax. The majority of crustaceans have appendages sticking out from their sides, which they use for walking or swimming. In some, the front pair bears pincers. Each appendage has two axes (ramii) and the main axis has five joints.

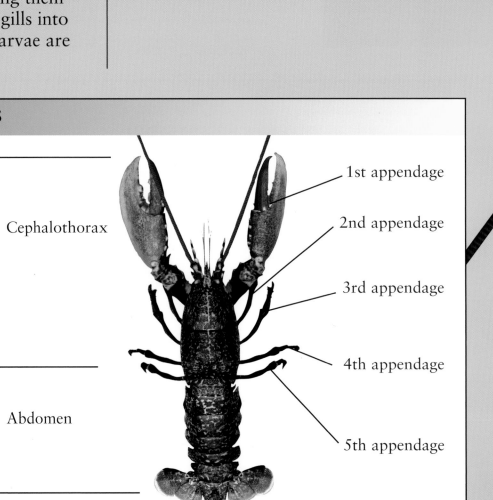

Cephalothorax

Abdomen

1st appendage

2nd appendage

3rd appendage

4th appendage

5th appendage

BRAIN

The small brain deals mainly with information from the antennae and eyes. A nerve cord running through the body controls most movement.

STOMACH

This muscular structure contains a "gastric mill" with hard "teeth" for grinding food. Bristles at the exit let small particles out but keep larger ones in.

Eyes

Rostrum

Mouth

TAIL MUSCLES

In lobsters, these are very powerful and flick the tail flippers when the animal needs to escape.

HEART AND BLOOD

The heart is a simple sac with one chamber. It pumps blood through arteries, each leading to a different part of the body. The blood then flows back to the heart via the gills where it picks up oxygen.

GILLS

In decapods such as lobsters, these feathery breathing structures are held beneath the shell at the tops of the legs. In many other crustaceans they stick out from the body.

Crushing
pincer

Cutting pincer

SMASH AND GRAB

The pincers carried by lobsters and crabs are used for feeding and defense. Most of these crustaceans are scavengers. Their claws help them crunch through shells and rip off pieces of flesh from the dead animals they eat. If they are threatened, they lift their claws up in front of them (right).

THE FIRST CRUSTACEANS

The origins of crustaceans are mysterious. Fossils tell us that they were around during the time of the dinosaurs, but they probably looked much different than present-day crustaceans.

SUDDEN ARRIVAL

The oldest crustacean fossils come from the Cambrian period, 540 million to 505 million years ago. They show seed shrimps that look very similar to those alive today. By the Devonian period, 410 million to 360 million years ago, the first shrimplike decapod crustaceans had appeared. They were followed in the late permian period, about 250 million years ago, by lobsters and crayfish. The oldest fossils of hermit crabs and true crabs come from rocks formed during the Jurassic period, 210 million to 145 million years ago.

ANCIENT LOBSTER
Evidence of early crustaceans comes from fossils.
The large pincers can be seen clearly.

LOST COUSINS

Because the oldest crustacean fossils look like modern animals, scientists can only guess which group they evolved from. The ancient animals that look most like crustaceans belonged to a group called the Phosphatocopina. These creatures, which lived in the early Cambrian period, looked similar to seed shrimps, but are now extinct. Other extinct relatives of the crustaceans include the trilobites.

TRILOBITES

These extinct creatures were once among the most common animals on Earth. They lived on the seabed, and some grew to 28 inches (71 cm) long. Like many crustaceans, trilobites had a segmented abdomen and a cephalothorax covered by a single shell.

Trilobites lived in all of the world's seas. They died out about 250 million years ago.

GETTING AROUND

Crustaceans move mainly by using their limbs, although some have other methods of getting around. Most crustaceans can either walk or swim, and many can do both. A few species burrow.

WALKING

Lobsters and crabs get around on foot. Their long, jointed legs can carry them surprisingly quickly. Ghost crabs may clock up to 4 miles (6.4 km) per hour as they scuttle over beaches. Crabs and lobsters have legs that end in sharp tips. These help them to grip the surface as they move along. Lobsters find it easy to lift their bodies off the ground because the seawater they live in provides buoyancy, helping them float. On land, it takes more effort. Crabs have smaller, more rounded, lighter bodies.

The other main group of crustaceans that move by walking are sow bugs. They have seven pairs of legs, which are quite short and almost hidden beneath them.

SIDE STEPPING
Although most crabs can walk forward and backward, they find it quickest to move sideways. This is because of the way their legs are jointed and the direction in which they bend.

OUT OF ITS ELEMENT
Crayfish normally live in freshwater, but they can creep over land if the pools they inhabit dry up.

VELVET SWIMMING CRAB

When they are not hiding in crevices, these crabs spend most of their time walking over the seabed in search of food. They use the paddles on their rear legs to help them escape danger, swimming away rapidly if attacked.

SWIMMING

The majority of crustaceans live in water, and swimming is the main way they get around. Many of these crustaceans have paddlelike appendages called swimmerets that stick out from under the abdomen. Prawns have these as well as legs. Other, smaller, crustaceans use all of their appendages for swimming. Each of their limbs has long, protruding hairlike structures, which catch the water and push them along.

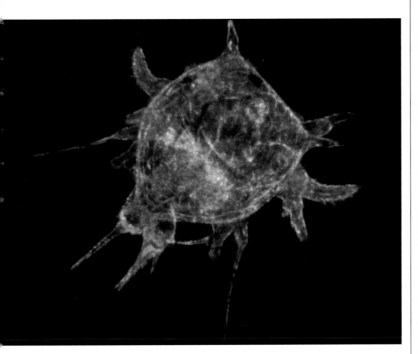

TINY MOVER

Crustacean larvae float at the mercy of the currents. This young barnacle can swim, but is too small and weak to move far on its own.

SAND HOPPERS

These creatures are closely related to freshwater shrimps. They use their legs to clamber around the rotting seaweed they feed on. However, if they are disturbed, they can suddenly spring into the air, propelled by a flick of their tails.

Sand hoppers are very common on some beaches, especially near the high-tide mark.

17

SENSES

Crustaceans experience the world through a number of senses. The most important of these are vision and touch.

COMPOUND EYES

Most decapods have excellent vision. Their eyes contain hundreds of tiny square sides, arranged across the surface in a pattern like graph paper. These focus incoming light by reflection, directing it onto the sensitive tissue of the retina. Our own eyes also have a retina but refract light onto it using a lens.

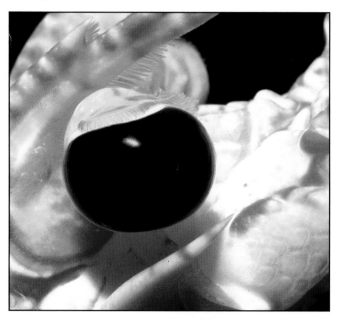

BEADY EYE

A prawn's compound eye enables it to see in almost every direction at once.

ON THE LOOKOUT

Many crustaceans have their eyes on stalks. Hermit crabs and some other crabs can move these stalks separately, folding them down to protect the eyes when necessary.

SUPERSIGHT

Mantis shrimps have the finest color vision in the entire animal kingdom. While our eyes only have three types of cells to perceive color in the "visible" spectrum, theirs have eight. On top of that, they have four other types of cells that can detect ultraviolet light, something that humans cannot see at all. It is these different detector cells that let them see such a wide variety of colors.

LIFE IN THE DARK

Although some crustaceans have very good eyesight, others rely on their sense of touch to find their way around. Many crustaceans come out at night to search for food or live in water so deep that no light reaches them. For these crustaceans, the sense of touch is enhanced by antennae. These "feelers" amplify movements in the water and enable them to detect what is ahead before they actually bump into it.

Many crustaceans have a good sense of smell. This is most important for scavengers, such as lobsters, because it helps them find dead animals to feed on.

FLEXIBLE FEELERS

A lobster's antennae, like its other appendages, are jointed and can be moved to point in all directions. Some lobsters have antennae that are longer than the rest of their entire bodies.

Sow bugs have small, relatively simple eyes that can tell the difference between light and dark, but do not allow them to see detail. They rely on smell to find their way around.

Sow bugs use their antennae to smell the world rather than feel it. Each of the jointed appendages sprouting from their heads has its own nostril. Smell is important to sow bugs since they spend most of their time in the dark. Despite the fact that they live on land and are active by day, they rarely see sunlight. They inhabit the leaf litter and rotting logs on forest floors, squeezing through dark gaps to find their food.

FOOD AND FEEDING

Crustaceans eat a range of food. They can be scavengers, suspension feeders, or parasites, living on other animals and eating their body tissues.

OCEAN VULTURES

The best known crustaceans, crabs and lobsters, live mainly on carrion. They scour the seabed for dead animals, which drift down from the waters above. Many prawns are also scavengers, while cephalocarids eat the organic matter that builds up in mud.

One whole group of crustaceans has evolved into parasites. Fish lice live on the skin and in the gill cavities of their hosts, drawing their body fluids and small pieces of flesh up through their sucking mouthparts.

DEAD MEAT

The American lobster lives in the western Atlantic Ocean, where it searches the sea floor for carrion. It uses its pincers to pull apart its find.

ANYTHING LEFT?

The mouthparts of lobsters and crabs are quite small and can only handle small pieces of food. Small creatures are picked up with the pincers and held next to the mouth for feeding.

SMALL PORTIONS

Some crustaceans feed on plankton. Krill collect microscopic algae using legs covered with fine hairs. Other plankton eaters also sift their food from the water. All of the world's barnacles feed in this way.

On dry land, sow bugs eat rotting vegetation. Water slaters, close relatives of sow bugs, feed on leaves that fall into the ponds and rivers they inhabit.

CLEANING SERVICE

Cleaner shrimps eat parasites and bits of dead skin, which they pick off fish. Many fish actually seek out the shrimps and let them clamber all over their bodies, sometimes even opening their gill covers since they are unable to clean themselves.

Some cleaner shrimps gather at "cleaning stations" where they wait for their clients.

SUSPENSION FEEDERS

Goose barnacles gather tiny particles of food using their feathery cirri. Cirri are modified legs that the barnacles use to sweep through the water. Every so often, the cirri are pulled back in to transfer any trapped food into the mouth.

The urge to breed is a driving force in the crustacean life cycle. Adults often go far out of their way and travel long distances to find a partner. Some show off or fight one another to win the attention of mates.

LOOK AT ME!
Male fiddler crabs have one claw that is much larger than the other. They use this to attract females and warn other males to stay away from their patch of beach. If another male approaches, these crabs will attack.

PAIRING UP

Most adult crustaceans are either male or female and can only reproduce by mating with a partner of the opposite sex. There are some exceptions; for example, most barnacles are both male and female at once and can reproduce by themselves. In a few crustacean species, the females can produce young without mating at all. Normally, however, finding a partner is vital. To make it easier, most crustaceans breed at particular times of the year.

CRAB COUPLE
In many crustaceans, the females are much bigger than the males. These spider crabs are courting, getting used to each other before actually mating.

CARING PARENTS

Many female crustaceans guard their eggs until they hatch and actually carry them around for safekeeping. Most female crabs, lobsters, and freshwater crayfish carry their young. Some crustaceans, such as copepods and mysid shrimps, have special brood pouches on their bodies, which hold the eggs until they hatch. Mysid shrimps are also known as opposum shrimps.

The eggs of a female crayfish are clearly visible under its abdomen.

STRANGE BEHAVIOR

Some crustaceans change sex as they get older. When they are young, they are males, but as they grow, they become females. They change because the female produces large numbers of eggs, which are much bigger than the sperm that fertilize them. A bigger body can carry more eggs. Species that change sex include caridean shrimps.

Other crustaceans change the way they breed to react to surrounding conditions. Daphnia, water fleas, are tiny freshwater crustaceans. When there is plenty of space, they are all female and produce clones of themselves. But if the pool shrinks, they start to produce male young. These mate with the females, which then lay eggs that can survive for a while if the pool dries up.

GROWING UP

Most young crustaceans look nothing like their parents. What is more, they live very different lives, floating free as part of the plankton. It is only later that they start to change.

ALTERED BEASTS
When the first crustacean larvae were discovered, many were described as completely new species. In some cases, it was decades before it was realized that they were actually the young of creatures that had already been named. Almost all marine crustaceans have planktonic larvae. Some stay in the plankton for up to a year.

PRAWN ZOEA
All decapod crustaceans hatch out as zoea. Many stay in this form until they change into adults. Zoea have compound eyes and a thorax made up of segments.

THREE OF A KIND
There are three main types of crustacean larvae. Most groups have young that hatch as nauplii. These have a single eye and a body shaped like a shield with mouthparts and antennae, which are used for swimming. As they grow, they molt and each time they do this, segments and appendages are added to their bodies. The other two types of larvae, zoea and megalops, are only produced by decapods.

CRAB MEGALOPS
Megalops larvae develop from zoea and are an intermediate stage in crab development. After living as megalops, crabs change into their adult form.

BREAKING OUT

Crustaceans have to molt in order to grow. They break out of their old shell and take in water to pump themselves up before their new shell hardens. Molting is risky since the soft body is vulnerable.

ALL CHANGE

As crustacean larvae grow older, they start to look more and more like their parents. Eventually, they change into miniature versions of the adult form and take on the adult animal's lifestyle. Although they are now young adults, they continue to grow, their bodies expanding inside their hard shells. When they reach a certain size and cannot grow any larger inside their present shell, they are forced to break out of it and form a new, larger one. This process is known as molting.

LIKE FATHER LIKE SON

Although they molt and grow, sow bugs have the same form throughout their life cycle.

Sow bugs are an exception to the usual crustacean rule. Their young hatch out fully formed, like tiny adults. Female sow bugs carry their eggs around with them until they hatch, keeping them in a special pouch underneath their bodies. Once they have hatched, the young start their own independent lives.

GROUPS

Crustaceans gather for different reasons. Some form groups to be near a particular food source, others because they have gathered to mate. A few species make journeys in very large numbers.

FOOD FOR ALL

Soldier crabs inhabit Australia's coastal mudflats. They form "armies" as they move over the mud at low tide, picking out particles of food.

CRUSTACEAN COLONIES

The main reason crustaceans form colonies is food. These creatures gather not because of the advantages of living together but simply because there is enough food to support large numbers of them. Some barnacles, for example, form colonies on seashore rocks. Here, the tide brings them lots of food for which there is little or no competition. Their tough shells allow them to survive both in and out of the water.

GATHERING TO BREED

Many crustaceans only breed at certain times. To increase their chances of finding a partner, some head for particular places, where they gather in large numbers. Every August, for example, spider crabs group together to breed in one spot off the coast of Dorset in Britain. In some years, as many as 50,000 spider crabs have gathered.

RED CRAB MIGRATION

Every November, Christmas Island in the Indian Ocean suddenly becomes covered with red crabs. As many as 100 million of these little crustaceans emerge from their burrows across the island to march down to the shore to breed. The migration is led by the mature males, which fight among themselves for the best mating burrows before the females arrive. Once they have paired up and mated, the males leave the beaches and head back inland. The females then wait two weeks for their eggs to develop. Then they head down to the water's edge and release them into the sea.

Up to a million red crabs are killed every year on the roads of Christmas Island as they make their annual breeding migration. After 25 days developing in the sea, an army of baby red crabs emerges on the island's beaches before heading inland to dig burrows and set up homes of their own.

MASS MIGRATIONS
Some crustaceans make journeys together in large groups. Female blue crabs, for instance, travel from the Rhode River down to the mouth of Chesapeake Bay. They do this because their larvae need salt to develop properly. The females mate with their partners and then feed in the fresher water around the river mouth.

FOLLOW THE LEADER
Caribbean spiny lobsters march in single file across the seabed every fall. They do this to reach deeper waters, which are warmer in winter.

27

CRABS AND LOBSTERS

To most people, crabs and lobsters are the classic crustaceans, perhaps because they include the largest crustaceans of all.

WHAT IS THE DIFFERENCE?

Both crabs and lobsters are decapods, crustaceans with 10 limbs. Most lobsters and all crabs have pincers, but lobsters have a long, segmented abdomen that sticks out at the back of their bodies. Crabs have a similar abdomen, but it is smaller and is curled up underneath the the main "shell."

HIDEY HOLE

Many crabs have flat bodies that enable them to squeeze into very narrow crevices. Some stay hidden during the day and only come out at night to feed.

WHERE DO THEY LIVE?

All the world's lobsters live in the sea. Crayfish, which look very similar to lobsters, live in freshwater. Crabs, on the other hand, live in a much wider variety of habitats. Some spend nearly all of their lives on land, only returning to the water to breed. Others never leave the sea and a few live in fresh-water. The place most of us meet crabs is at the beach. Crabs are better adapted to shore life than almost any other animals.

LITTLE NIPPER

Crabs come in a huge variety of shapes and sizes. The tiny porcelain crab lives on tropical reefs, clambering over the coral in search of morsels of carrion.

Unlike true lobsters, slipper lobsters do not have pincers. Their flat, platelike antennae are also unique.

THE HARD SHELL

Large crabs and lobsters have few natural predators. Their hard exoskeleton protects them from all but the toughest jaws. Crustacean shells are made from chitin, reinforced with calcium carbonate. In these largest of all crustaceans, the shells are exceptionally thick. They provide not only protection, but also strength for the pincers, enabling them to crush and cut through most tissue.

BIG HAND

Lobsters feed mainly on carrion, but they also capture some live prey. The pincers of some species are enormous. In the largest, such as the North Atlantic lobster, they may account for 45 percent of the total body weight.

HERMIT CRABS

While most crabs rely on their own shells for protection, hermit crabs are extra cautious. They hide their bodies inside the empty shells of dead mollusks, such as periwinkles, which they carry with them wherever they go. Hermit crabs have soft, twisted abdomens to fit into the shells they inhabit. Their pincers are massive and are used to block the entrance to the shell, which the crab retreats into if attacked.

As hermit crabs grow, they have to find and move into new, bigger shells.

PRAWNS AND SHRIMPS

Prawns and shrimps are the most numerous of large crustaceans. Like crabs and lobsters, they have 10 limbs, but their pincers are smaller.

WHAT'S IN A NAME?

The words *prawn* and *shrimp* mean different things in different parts of the world. From a scientific point of view, they are interchangeable. Zoologists group these crustaceans into several families, each defined by subtle differences in body structure and its own Latin name.

COMMON PRAWN

This species is widespread around the coasts of Britain and Europe. Like many prawns and shrimps, it is omnivorous, feeding on a wide range of living and dead organic matter.

KRILL

These shrimplike creatures live in the seas around Antarctica. In the short polar summer they form vast swarms, several billion strong. These swarms support an entire food chain, feeding everything from penguins to whales.

Individual krill are about 2 inches (5 cm) long.

GOING PLACES

Shrimps and prawns have a lot in common with lobsters. Like them, they have long bodies ending with a fan-shaped tail. This is made up of five segments and used for escape, propelling its owner rapidly backward through the water. Shrimps and prawns normally swim using the small swimmerets on their underside. They also have legs for walking on the seabed.

CLEAR VIEW

Some shrimps have virtually transparent bodies with patches of pigment at the surface.

MANTIS SHRIMPS

Mantis shrimps are not actually decapods, but they are closely related to true shrimps. Mantis shrimps hunt small prey on the seabed with an unusual method of attack. They club prey to death with a powerful punch from their front limbs. The punch of a mantis shrimp is so powerful that it can smash through glass. When they are kept in tanks, reinforced glass has to be used.

Most mantis shrimps are a few inches long, but the largest can reach 16 inches (40 cm) long.

STRANGE PARTNERS

Most prawns and shrimps are solitary creatures, but a few spend their lives with unusual partners. One group of blind shrimps live side by side with small fish called gobies. The shrimp digs and maintains a burrow, which both creatures share. In return, the goby keeps lookout for danger. Another group of shrimps live among the stinging tentacles of sea anemones. Each individual shrimp has its own anemone, which it hides in for protection from predators.

HARLEQUIN SHRIMP
Harlequin shrimps live on reefs and feed almost entirely on starfish and sea urchins. Each shrimp has its own unique pattern.

BARNACLES

Not many people realize that barnacles are crustaceans. Unlike their relatives, these creatures spend their adult lives fixed to one spot, sifting the water around them for food.

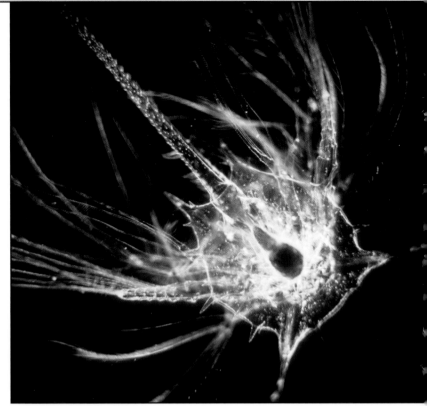

NAUPLIUS LARVA

At this early stage, barnacles look like many other larval crustaceans. They have two small antennae, several swimming appendages, and a single eye, the dark spot in the middle of the body.

YOUNG AND FREE

As larvae, barnacles live like many other immature crustaceans, swimming free in the plankton. After hatching within the safety of their parents' shells, they are released into the water as tiny nauplius larvae. Each adult barnacle may release more than 10,000 larvae.

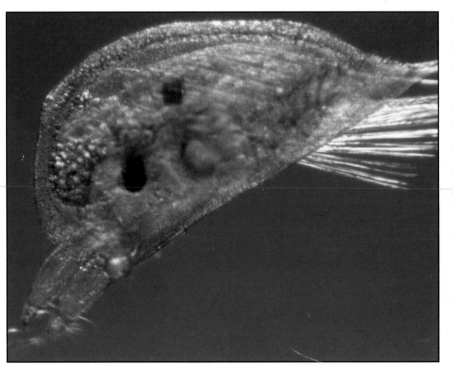

CYPRIS LARVA

The body of a barnacle cypris larva is contained within a hinged carapace. Its thick antennae stick out from one end (left).

SETTLING DOWN

Most barnacle nauplius larvae live in the plankton for two months, feeding on microscopic algae. During this time, they go through several molts, eventually changing form to become cypris larvae. When this happens they stop feeding and start the search for somewhere to settle. Special touch and chemical receptors help them locate suitable areas and adults of their own species. Having found a good spot, they release a sticky mass from glands in their antennae and attach themselves to it.

GOOSE BARNACLES

Unlike most adult barnacles, which have their shells and bodies virtually fused to the surface they live on, goose barnacles are connected by a leathery stalk. Their bodies are protected by a case of five glossy white plates.

Many goose barnacles live in different areas from other barnacles and sometimes attach themselves to driftwood or make their own floats with hardened bubbles.

Goose barnacles were named in medieval times when they were thought to grow into geese.

FIXED ABODE

Adult barnacles feed by waiting for prey to come to them. They sweep it from the water using feathery feeding legs called cirri. To breed, barnacles either fertilize themselves or a close neighbor. They then brood the eggs inside their shells, out of reach of any predators.

WELL PROTECTED

Most barnacles are surrounded by plates of calcium carbonate. Two are hinged and can open. The others fuse to form a cone-shaped case.

33

Sow Bugs

Small and inconspicuous, sow bugs are surprisingly widespread. These little creatures are found in a wide range of land habitats. Some even have colonized human homes.

A LOT OF ROT

Sow bugs are sometimes called wood lice or pill bugs. They are the only true land crustaceans, spending their entire lives out of water. Sow bugs feed on rotting plant matter and are particularly common on forest floors. They also live in parks and gardens, where they can usually be found under fallen wood, rocks, or stones.

SAFETY PROCEDURE

Some sow bugs can roll into a ball to protect themselves, hiding their legs and other vulnerable parts. Most species also taste unpleasant, so larger predators, such as mice, rarely eat them.

DARK AND DAMP

Although they live on land, sow bugs have gills and must stay damp to survive. This is why they are rarely seen. They tend to avoid direct sunlight and usually only come out from their hiding places at night. Although most sow bugs look quite similar there are actually many different species. Experts can tell them apart by their size and the texture of their carapace.

ARMOR PLATED

The hinged carapace of a sow bug keeps it well protected from most insects and other small predators, such as spiders.

CLOSE RELATIVES

Sow bugs are classified by scientists as part of the order Isopoda. Other members of this crustacean group have similar body features but often have very different lifestyles. One isopod that lives in a similar way to sow bugs is the sea slater. It hides under rocks near the high-tide mark on

beaches and scavenges for food in washed debris. Sea slaters are slightly bigger than sow bugs and move much faster. Most other isopods inhabit the ocean. Some of these creatures are microscopic, but others grow up to 16 inches (40 cm) long.

MARINE ISOPOD

Some sea isopods are scavengers. Others feed on seaweed, and a few are predators. Many isopods live in very deep water. Their relatives, the amphipods, live even farther down. The deepest living animal is an amphipod, Hirondellea gigas. It exists at depths of 31,824 feet (9,700 m).

WATER SLATERS

Unlike most water creatures, water slaters are poor swimmers, preferring to clamber over pondweed or walk over the bottom of the freshwater pools they live in. They feed on rotting vegetation, including the leaves that drop into ponds from trees.

Water slaters look similar to sow bugs but have longer legs.

OTHER CRUSTACEANS

Many crustaceans are so tiny that they are rarely noticed. However, they make up a large part of the plankton and form a vital link in both marine and freshwater food chains.

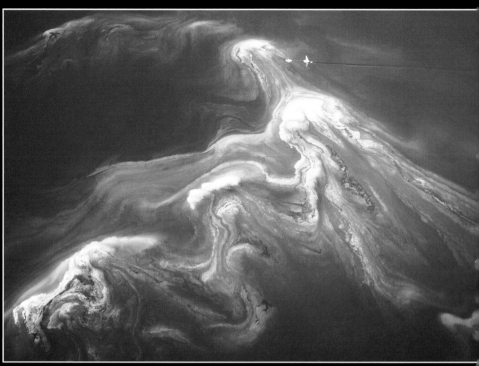

LIVING SOUP
Plankton are the tiny animals and algae that drift through bodies of water. Many of these organisms are invisible to the naked eye and can only be seen using a microscope. Most crustaceans have planktonic larvae, but a large number spend their adult lives in the plankton as well. Some feed on the algae and others are hunters.

PLANKTON BLOOM SEEN FROM THE AIR
Usually planktonic organisms are invisible to our eyes, lost in the water. Every so often, however, they gather and reproduce in such huge numbers that they change the color of the sea. This phenomenon is known as a plankton bloom.

SEED SHRIMPS

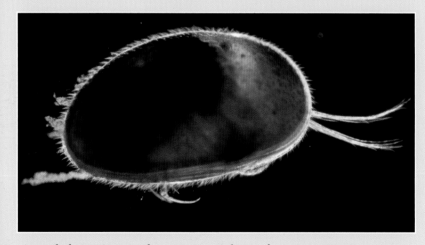

A seed shrimp's paired antennae stick out from its carapace.

These crustaceans live within the two halves of a hinged carapace, like tiny mussels. They move by means of feathery appendages, which barely stick out of the bottom. This makes them look like swimming seeds. If they sense danger, seed shrimps can snap the two halves of their carapace together. Some marine seed shrimps grow to 1 inch (2.5 cm) long, but most freshwater species are much smaller.

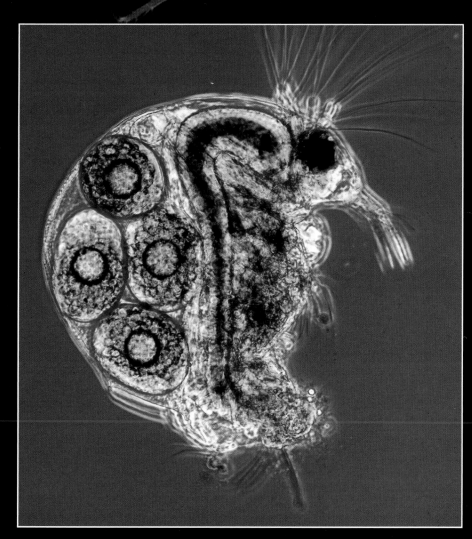

COPEPOD

These tiny marine crustaceans feed on algae and are themselves an important food source for fish. This copepod has been magnified thousands of times and colored to show its parts. Its antennae are green.

TINY LIVES

Most of the world's freshwater crustaceans are branchiopods. The largest members of this group are fairy shrimps, some of which may reach 4 inches (10 cm) long. Most branchiopods are smaller, however, and include water fleas. Some branchiopods live as part of the marine plankton, alongside the much more numerous copepods. Mystacocarids are still little known. This is partly because of their small size and partly because of where they live—between grains of sand. Cephalocarids are also poorly understood. They are also tiny but live in soft marine sediments.

WATER FLEA

Freshwater branchiopods feed on bacteria and other tiny living things. They move by beating their feathery antennae. Water fleas' bodies are naturally transparent, showing all of their internal organs. This one is also carrying four eggs.

37

HORSESHOE CRABS

Bizarre, alien, prehistoric. All of these words seem appropriate for the horseshoe crabs, armored survivors from an older, more primitive Earth.

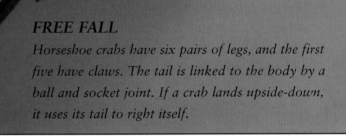

SHARED ANCESTRY

Horseshoe crabs are not true crabs at all. In fact, they are not even crustaceans. Zoologists have given horseshoe crabs their own separate class named Merostomata, and this only includes five living species. Their closest relatives are the crustaceans and the arachnids. Many millions of years ago, all three of these invertebrate groups evolved from one common ancestor.

FREE FALL

Horseshoe crabs have six pairs of legs, and the first five have claws. The tail is linked to the body by a ball and socket joint. If a crab lands upside-down, it uses its tail to right itself.

LIVING FOSSILS

Horseshoe crabs have hardly changed since the age of the dinosaurs. The reason for this lack of change is their successful design. Evolution only acts on animals when changing conditions make their old body designs inefficient or uncompetitive. Horseshoe crabs have always been able to hold their own against newer animals and so have never needed to change.

ANCIENT EVIDENCE

This fossil comes from the Jurassic period, when dinosaurs walked the earth. It shows how little horseshoe crabs have changed. Those around then were almost identical to the ones alive today.

LIVING TANKS

Horseshoe crabs look like walking pieces of armor. They can be 2 feet (60 cm) long, including the tail. Despite their fearsome appearance, horseshoe crabs are quite harmless. They eat worms and other small animals from the seabed.

SOLID DEFENSES

Horseshoe crabs live on the seabed in shallow coastal waters. Their domed bodies make them very hard to attack. A horseshoe crab's exoskeleton is made entirely from chitin. Those of other crustaceans contain calcium carbonate.

BEACH INVASION

Horseshoe crabs leave the sea to breed. They emerge in late spring around the new and full moons—when the tide is highest—to deposit their eggs on particular beaches. They then return to the sea. Horseshoe crabs' eggs develop in the sand, hatching after five weeks. At the next full or new moon tide, when the sea reaches them, they leave the sand and swim to deeper water.

Horseshoe crabs lay their eggs on beaches to protect them from predators.

CRUSTACEAN GIANTS

GIANT STEPS

The Japanese spider crab has the longest legs of any crustacean. The biggest one ever caught had a leg span of more than 12 feet (3.6 m). Although truly massive, this species is not the heaviest. That title is held by the giant crab, which has a bulkier body.

Most crustaceans are tiny creatures but a few are giants. The largest are the biggest arthropods of all. Among invertebrates, only certain marine mollusks are bigger.

HEAVYWEIGHT CHAMPIONS

If weight is the true measure of size, then the North Atlantic lobster is the largest crustacean of all. This monster can reach more than 44 pounds (20 kg), which is heavier than the average 5-year-old child. The heaviest crab, simply known as the giant crab, comes from the Pacific Ocean and can weigh up to 31 pounds (14 kg).

KING PRAWN

These crustaceans include some of the largest prawns of all. This species, the western king prawn, lives off Australia and can grow to 8 inches (20 cm) long.

ROBBER CRAB

This is the largest land-living crustacean. It can weigh up to 9 pounds (4 kg) and has a leg span of 3 feet (.9 m). Robber crabs belong to the same group as hermit crabs, and the young actually carry shells for protection. As they get older, they discard these, and their own shell hardens over their abdomen. Like all crabs, they spend their larval stages in water, the females laying their eggs in the sea.

Robber crabs use their powerful pincers to break open coconuts and feed on the soft flesh inside.

OLD MASTERS

Crustaceans continue to grow throughout life, so the biggest individuals are usually the oldest. Giant crabs are believed to live to be at least 25 years old, and the largest may be over 40. Lobsters also can live to a great age. Scientists think that North Atlantic lobsters can live for at least 50 years. Although age is an important factor in crustacean size, their diet is also important. Crustaceans kept in captivity often get more food than in the wild, making them grow faster.

SEA MONSTER
The giant crab is fished commercially off Tasmania and the southern coast of Australia.

CRUSTACEANS AND US

People have eaten crustaceans for centuries. Most of us are more likely to see these creatures on our plates than alive. On the other hand, some people keep crustaceans as pets.

SEAFOOD STAPLES

Lobster thermidor, prawn cocktail, and paella are foods we may have heard of and many of us have tasted. The fact that these dishes are so familiar shows how popular crustaceans are as food. Crustaceans, along with mollusks such as mussels, are included on restaurant menus as shellfish, even though they are not fish at all. Fishing for crustaceans is big business in some parts of the world. Not all the crustaceans we eat come from the wild. Many of them are farmed instead, particularly the edible prawns and shrimps.

BOILED ALIVE

Some people argue that the way lobsters are cooked is cruel. They are dropped into boiling water while still alive and do not die instantly. As they are cooked, their shells turn red.

SIZZLING SHELLFISH

In Australia, freshwater crayfish are known as yabbies and are often cooked on barbecues.

AMERICAN FAVORITE

The blue crab lives on the east coast of the United States and is caught in large numbers for food. One of the main fisheries is around Chesapeake Bay, shared by Virginia and Maryland.

TAKING TOO MUCH?

Most crustaceans are common, but they can be threatened by overfishing. The creatures that feed on them can suffer even more. The Hawaiian monk seal, for example, has been pushed to the edge of extinction by overfishing of lobsters, its main prey. Not all crustaceans are caught for humans to eat. Most krill are used in animal feed. Overfishing for krill in the Antarctic has led to concern about the penguin and whale population.

ON THE OUTSIDE LOOKING IN
Crabs and lobsters are caught with a variety of baited traps. These are dropped to the seabed but are linked to a floating buoy on the surface.

COLLECTIBLE CRUSTACEANS

Some people keep crustaceans for a hobby. Tropical reef species are particularly popular with aquarists, who keep them with saltwater fish in glass tanks. Some people breed these crustaceans for sale but others collect them from the wild. Collecting crustaceans can cause problems to reef ecosystems. Overcollection can even endanger these species in the wild.

Indo-Pacific white banded cleaner shrimps are collected in large numbers for home aquariums.

ANIMAL CLASSIFICATION

The animal kingdom can be split into two main groups, vertebrates (with a backbone) and invertebrates (without a backbone). From these two main groups, scientists classify, or sort, animals further based on their shared characteristics.

The six main groupings of animals, from the most general to the most specific, are: phylum, class, order, family, genus, and species. This system was created by Carolus Linnaeus.

To see how this system works, follow the example of how human beings are classified in the vertebrate group and how earthworms are classified in the invertebrate group.

ANIMAL KINGDOM

VERTEBRATE	INVERTEBRATE
PHYLUM: Chordata	**PHYLUM:** Annelida
CLASS: Mammals	**CLASS:** Oligochaeta
ORDER: Primates	**ORDER:** Haplotaxida
FAMILY: Hominids	**FAMILY:** Lumbricidae
GENUS: *Homo*	**GENUS:** *Lumbricus*
SPECIES: *sapiens*	**SPECIES:** *terrestris*

There are more than 30 groups of phyla. The nine most common are listed below along with their common name.

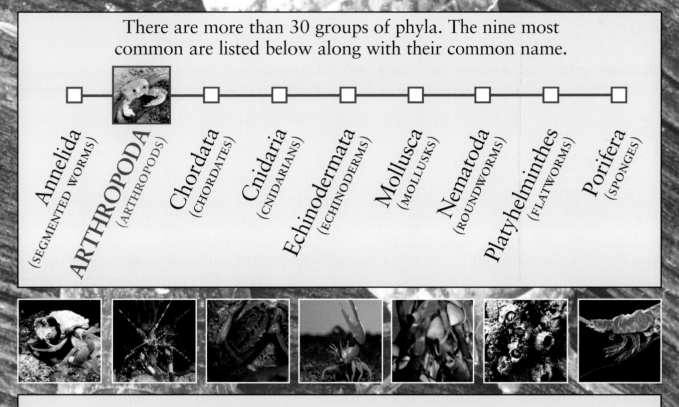

Annelida (SEGMENTED WORMS)

ARTHROPODA (ARTHROPODS)

Chordata (CHORDATES)

Cnidaria (CNIDARIANS)

Echinodermata (ECHINODERMS)

Mollusca (MOLLUSKS)

Nematoda (ROUNDWORMS)

Platyhelminthes (FLATWORMS)

Porifera (SPONGES)

This book highlights animals from the Arthropoda phylum. Follow the example below to learn how scientists classify the *Ocypode quadrata,* or the Atlantic ghost crab.

INVERTEBRATE

PHYLUM: Arthropoda

CLASS: Malacostraca

ORDER: Decapoda

FAMILY: Ocypodidae

GENUS: *Ocypode*

SPECIES: *quadrata*

Ocypode quadrata
(Atlantic ghost crab)

GLOSSARY

ABDOMEN
The part of the body that usually contains parts involved in digesting food, getting rid of waste, and breeding

ANTENNAE
The "feelers" on a crustacean's head

ARACHNIDS
The group of invertebrates that includes spiders and scorpions; all arachnids have eight legs

ARTHROPODS
Invertebrates with jointed legs; these include arachnids, crustaceans, and insects

CARAPACE
The upper shell of a crustacean

CARRION
The meat of an animal found when it is already dead

DECAPOD
A member of the order Decapoda. All decapods have 10 limbs; they include crabs, lobsters, prawns, and shrimps

EVOLUTION
The process by which new animals appear and change over time

EXOSKELETON
The tough outer covering of an arthropod's body

EXTINCT
A species that has died out forever

FOSSIL
The preserved remains of an animal or an impression in rock made by the body of an animal

GILLS
Structures used by animals to remove oxygen from water

HABITAT
The area or type of environment in which an animal naturally occurs

INVERTEBRATE
An animal without a backbone or spinal cord

LARVA
An animal's young, immature body form before it becomes an adult

MIGRATION
A long journey made by animals of the same species at the same time every year

PARASITE
An animal that lives on or inside another animal, giving nothing in return

PIGMENTS
Colored chemicals in an animal's skin

PLANKTON
Tiny animals and other living organisms that live suspended in water

PREDATOR
An animal that hunts others for food

PREY
An animal that is hunted by a predator

REPRODUCTION
The process by which a new generation of animals is created

SCAVENGER
An animal that feeds on carrion

THORAX
The middle part of the body of certain animals

Look for more Animal Kingdom books:

Tree Frogs, Mud Puppies & Other Amphibians
ISBN 0-7565-1249-2

Ant Lions, Wasps & Other Insects
ISBN 0-7565-1250-6

Peacocks, Penguins & Other Birds
ISBN 0-7565-1251-4

Angelfish, Megamouth Sharks & Other Fish
ISBN 0-7565-1252-2

Bats, Blue Whales & Other Mammals
ISBN 0-7565-1249-2

Centipedes, Millipedes, Scorpions & Spiders
ISBN 0-7565-1254-9

Dwarf Geckos, Rattlesnakes & Other Reptiles
ISBN 0-7565-1255-7

Snails, Shellfish & Other Mollusks
ISBN 0-7565-1613-7

Starfish, Urchins & Other Echinoderms
ISBN 0-7565-1611-0

Nematodes, Leeches & Other Worms
ISBN 0-7565-1615-3

Sponges, Jellyfish & Other Simple Animals
ISBN 0-7565-1614-5

FURTHER RESOURCES

AT THE LIBRARY
Debelius, Helmut. *Crustacea Guide of the World*. Hollywood Import & Export Inc., 1999.

Mente, Elena. *Nutrition, Physiology, and Metabolism of Crustaceans*. Enfield, NH: Science Publishers, Inc., 2002.

Murray, Peter. *Mollusks and Crustaceans*. Chanhassen, MN: Child's World, 2004.

Pascoe, Elaine. *Crabs*. Woodbridge, CT: Blackbirch Press, 2005.

ON THE WEB
For more information on *crustaceans*, use FactHound to track down Web sites related to this book.
1. Go to *www.facthound.com*
2. Type in a search word related to this book or this book ID: 0756516129
3. Click on the *Fetch It* button FactHound will find the best Web sites for you.

INDEX